Of Bells and Cells

The World of Monks, Friars, Sisters and Nuns

Written by M. Cristina Borges

Illustrated by Michaela Harrison

ST. BONOSA BOOKS

Nihil Obstat: Very Reverend Monsignor Chanel Jeanty
            Chancellor & Vicar General

Imprimatur: ✠ Most Reverend Thomas G. Wenski
            Archbishop of Miami
            June 8, 2016

St. Bonosa Books
info@stbonosabooks.com
www.stbonosabooks.com
© 2013, 2020, 2021 by M. Cristina Borges

Cover Design: Michaela Harrison

Original English: *Of Bells and Cells*
25 24 23 22 21 1 2 3 4 5

ISBN: 978-0-9906560-6-7 (USA/CAN hardcover)

Other Editions and Translations:
ISBN: 978-0-6159075-8-1 (USA/CAN paperback)
ISBN: 978-0-9906560-0-5 (GB/IRE/AUS paperback)
ISBN: 978-0-9906560-8-1 - *De claustros y campanas* (ES paperback)
ISBN: 978-0-9906560-9-8 - *De claustros y campanas* (ES hardcover)
ISBN: 978-0-9906560-3-6 (FR) - *Cloche et cloître*
ISBN: 978-65-89415-28-2 (POR) - *Um chamado especial* (Centro Dom Bosco)
ISBN: 978-80-87865-38-8 (CZ) - *Zvony a kutny* (Kartuziánské nakladatelství)
ISBN: 978-91-85608-77-5 (SV) - *Om klockor och kloster* (Bokförlaget Catholica)

Printed in the United States of America, Great Britain, and Australia

ehind this little book is much more than meets the eye. Into it went a lot of prayer and labor. From the bottom of our hearts, we thank all our dear religious friends—monks, nuns, friars and sisters—who prayed for its progress and completion, and who also read, suggested, corrected and encouraged us along the way. We will not mention any names, as we know they did it all for the glory of God, and as good religious they would much rather opt for self-effacing anonymity. They will read their own names hidden in these lines, and hopefully know how grateful we are and how much we admire and love them. Our heartfelt gratitude also to our dear families, who likewise contributed with their prayers and sacrifices and help in many ways. May this joint labor of ours bear much fruit for His glory and the good of souls.

God created us to know, serve, and love Him on
this earth and to be happy with Him for all Eternity
in Heaven.

We know God by learning about Him and about all that Holy Mother Church teaches, and by praying and talking to Him. We serve Him by doing His will. And we love Him because He loves us and has done everything for us! God knows each one of us individually, from each little strand of hair on our head, down to each tiny thought in our mind and each tiny stirring of our heart. He knows what is best for us, and has a Will and Call for each one of us in this life.

Many He calls to grow up, marry, have children and form a family. Fathers and mothers are called to sacrifice many little, and many big things, and to give of themselves to their children, helping them to grow, to learn, and to love God.

Others receive a special call: they are called to grow up and live life already here on earth as it is lived by all in Heaven. There in Heaven, as Jesus said, we are like angels, neither giving nor taking in marriage. Priests, monks, friars, nuns and sisters are called to this special way of life. They live a life of total dedication and self-giving to God, a life of undivided attention to Him. They also form big families of their own—religious families, called "religious orders," living together in community inside "monasteries" or "convents" under the care and guidance of a "superior."

Just as in a family, grandfather and grandmother pass on name, looks, and ways to father and mother, and then father and mother pass on name, looks, and ways to their children, so religious families pass on—from one generation to the next—a way of living, praying, and of thinking about God.

Those people who have a calling to join a religious order and follow this special way of life are said to have a "vocation" to religious life. ("Vocation" comes from the word *vocare* in the Latin language, which means "to call" or "to summon.") And they are called "religious."

But whether God calls one to be married . . .

. . . or to remain single and serve Him . . .

. . . or to be a religious or a priest . . .

. . . He calls everyone to be a **SAINT**. And He gives each one of us the grace needed to become a saint in his or her own calling.

Sometimes little children will feel, early in their lives, that they are being called by God to be a religious, to follow this special way of life of dedicated service to Our Lord. Others won't realize that they have a religious vocation until much later in life. But usually, it is when a young man or woman is around 18 years of age to about 25 that he or she will leave home to start the new life of a religious with their new, religious family.

The first six months to a year are a period of introduction to their new way of life. During this time the newly entered young man or woman is called a "postulant." The word "postulant" comes from the Latin *postulare*, that is, "to request." A postulant is someone who has requested to enter a religious family or community. The postulant lives with the religious community—but not yet as a member—participating in all its activities: prayer, study, work and recreation. This period of postulancy permits the postulant to learn the community's ways, and thus to find out whether he or she is suited to that way of life and feels at home with that particular community. By the same token, during this time, the members of the community get to know the postulant and find out whether he or she is suited for their group. So the period of postulancy is a time during which both postulant and religious community get to know each other.

After the period of postulancy, if both postulant and community agree that he or she will be at home in that religious community and will be able to follow its rules and daily routine, the postulant officially enters the community and becomes a "novice." "Novice" comes from the Latin word *novus* or "new." A novice is a religious who is new, with little experience of the religious life; something like an "apprentice" who will now be trained—outwardly and inwardly—to become a better and better religious.

Outwardly, the novice will be trained in all the details of the day-to-day living of the religious community he or she joined: how to get up early in the morning at a set time every day, and to retire to one's cell (the religious's small room) to sleep at the same time every night (not too late); how to come to the chapel several times a day at the ring of a bell, and how to conduct oneself in chapel while praying and singing; how to eat in the refectory (usually in silence, listening to an edifying reading); how to scrub the floor, or plough the soil, or wash the windows, or shelve the books, or weed the vegetable garden, or build a garden shed . . . whatever may be the task the novice is assigned to do.

But all the outward actions are really only aids to the important work that the religious does inwardly, inside the soul—the long process, which lasts a lifetime, of "dying to self," that is, of not paying so much attention to ourselves so as to grow in the love of God and of neighbor.

Inwardly, the novice will learn how to keep the mind focused on the things of God, and how to pay attention to what goes on inside of his or her own heart. The religious must be always watchful against stirrings of pride, disobedience, sloth, and other "vices," and always looking for the opportunity to grow in the reverse "virtues," especially charity, humility, obedience and diligence. (In fact, this is what all of us must do, always.) In the measure that the religious "dies to self," that is, in the measure that the religious does not give in to those desires we have of having things our own way—of being noticed and admired by people, of getting the largest piece of cake, or keeping the most beautiful trinket—in that same measure, the novice will grow in the love of God, of Our Lady, of the saints in Heaven, the souls in Purgatory, and the souls still here on earth. In that measure, the novice will increase in the ability to do that which Our Lord asked of us—to pray always—and will act more and more in accordance with the Will of God. St. Paul said "Rejoice always, pray constantly, give thanks in all circumstances; for this is the will of God in Christ Jesus for you." (1 Thess. 5:16-18)

Novices are helped to learn all this by a teacher, called "novice master" in a men's community, or "novice mistress" in a women's community.

There is always a special ceremony through which the postulant becomes a novice, that is, when the postulant officially becomes a new member of the religious community. At this ceremony, the novice receives two very important signs: a new name and a "habit," or uniform.

In many religious communities, the novice is given a new name by the superior. This indicates that the novice has left the old self behind and has become a new person, about to begin a whole new life. The new name may have two parts: a first name preceded by "Brother" or "Sister," and a title, which is the novice's new surname, a sign that the novice now belongs to a religious family. In this manner, Jane Douglas becomes Sister Therese of the Holy Trinity, or Peter Torres becomes Brother Anthony of the Mother of God.

But, one of the clearest signs to the world that the former postulant is now a novice is that he or she now wears a "habit," the uniform worn by all the members of the particular religious order the novice has joined. Pope John Paul II said: "The Church must always seek to make her presence visible in everyday life, especially in contemporary culture, which is often very secularized and yet sensitive to the language of signs. In this regard, the Church has a right to expect a significant contribution from consecrated persons," and he goes on to add that religious ought to "wear their proper habit." (*Vita consecrata*, 1996)

Wearing a habit is one of the glories of religious life. It is a sign to everyone that this person wearing this special uniform is someone entirely dedicated to God, someone living apart from the world to pray for and serve

those who are in the world; a member of God's army who battles for the salvation of souls and who defends His Kingdom; a friend of God who keeps Him company at all times and seeks to please Him in all things (nuns wear a wedding ring and are said to be brides of Christ).

The habit is also a protection for the religious, outwardly and inwardly.

Outwardly, the habit inspires respect because people will know that the person wearing a habit is a religious. People will normally be inspired to behave well before a monk or a nun. But if the religious encounters a mean person, or someone who simply does not understand, and is mocked and made fun of, then the religious can do what our Lord said: "be glad and rejoice!" "Blessed are they that suffer persecution for justice's sake: for theirs is the Kingdom of Heaven. Blessed are you when they shall revile you, and persecute you, and speak all that is evil against you, untruly, for my sake: be glad and rejoice, for your reward is very great in Heaven for so they persecuted the prophets that were before you." (Mt. 5:10-12)

Inwardly, the habit gives protection as well. It can guard the religious against "vanity." By wearing the habit, religious do not have to think about how they look today, since they will always look the same every day, and they do not have to wonder whether their clothes are nicer and smarter than the others', since all members of a religious community dress alike. The habit even helps the religious give undivided attention to God: When monks, nuns,

friars and sisters wake up in the morning they take no time deciding what to wear that day since it is always their habit; so this is one less little instance of thinking of "self."

Each religious order has its own particular and distinct habit, so that not only does the habit tell the world that a person is a religious dedicated to God, but it also shows what religious order that person belongs to.

Now the novice, with the new name and the habit, will remain a novice for one, or two, or more years—a period of time called the "novitiate." The novice will stay in the novitiate until he or she is ready to make a commitment to fully embrace the religious life and to make serious promises to God about this commitment. Up till then, the novice lives and learns the life of a religious, and is a member of the religious community (no longer an observer, such as the postulant is). However, the novitiate is still a period during which the novice and his or her fellow religious can discern whether the novice truly has a vocation for the religious life as well as a calling to that particular religious order.

Toward the end of the novitiate, the senior members of the religious community have a meeting, called a "chapter," and decide whether the novice can become a full religious. That is, they will decide whether a novice can graduate, so to speak, from the novitiate—much like a graduation from college—and become a permanent member of the community.

So, to become a full and complete religious, the novice will make certain promises to God, which are forever . . .

Uscí-pe me Domi-ne, se cundum e-loqui-um tu-um et

Receive me O Lord, according to Thy word and I

The promises that the religious makes are called "vows." And there are usually three vows. All three tell God that the young man or woman making the profession of vows belongs fully and only to Him. They are . . .

THE VOW OF POVERTY

THE VOW OF CHASTITY

THE VOW OF OBEDIENCE

vi vam,   et non confundas me   ab exspecta-ti-o-ne me-a
will live, and do not permit that I fall from my hope.

    By the vow of Poverty, religious promise that they will have nothing of their own. This Poverty means that nothing belongs to them personally. Whatever they use is part of the belongings of the whole religious community. And the religious community is to be careful to have only simple and essential things.

    By taking the vow of Poverty, they tell God that they depend entirely on Him and His Divine Providence, that they trust in Him to provide for the necessities of life. It also keeps them from becoming too attached and worried about food, clothes, cars, books, tools, paintbrushes for themselves so that they are free to think of others.

Hint: for vow stories go to the end of the book.

Jesus said: "Behold the birds of the air, they neither sow, nor do they reap, nor gather into barns; and yet your Heavenly Father feeds them. . . . Consider the lilies of the field, how they grow; they neither toil nor spin; yet I tell you, even Solomon in all his glory was not arrayed [dressed] like one of these. . . . Therefore, do not be anxious saying, 'What shall we eat?' or 'What shall we drink?' or 'What shall we wear?' For the Gentiles seek all these things; and your Heavenly Father knows that you need them all. But seek first His Kingdom and his righteousness, and all these things shall be yours as well." (Mat. 6: 26, 28, 31-33)

The vow of Poverty, when properly lived, gives religious a great sense of joy and freedom, for they live out the fact that God is their Father and provides for every one of their needs, and so, they do not worry.

By the vow of Chastity, religious promise that they will be chaste and pure all their lives—just as everyone is called to be—but also that they will never marry.

Taking the vow of Chastity, they tell God that they belong to Him alone. Instead of having a husband or a wife, the religious will begin to live here on earth, the life of Heaven where, as Jesus said: ". . . they neither marry nor are given in marriage, but are like angels in Heaven." (Mt. 22:30)

They are those who the Lord said do not marry "for the sake of the Kingdom of Heaven" (Mt. 19:12). In this way they work to be as pure as the Virgin Mary, giving birth to Jesus in people's hearts.

The vow of Chastity, when lived properly, makes the love in the hearts of religious grow ever stronger and stronger, until all they can think of is how to go about pleasing God and helping others, so that they quite forget about themselves and are very happy.

By the vow of Obedience, religious promise that they will be obedient to their superiors and to the rules of their religious order, even if sometimes they do not understand or they find this hard to do. In this way, they tell God that they have complete trust in Him. By giving up their own self-will, they grow in one of the most important of virtues, which is humility. Also, in this way, by giving up their own self-will and promising to obey always, they allow God to act through their superiors.

For a religious, an order given by his or her superior is the same as an order given by God Himself, because of the vow of Obedience. God will not fail to honor this trust placed in Him by the religious through the vow of Obedience. "Trust in the Lord with all your heart, and lean not unto your own understanding. In all your ways acknowledge Him, and He shall direct your paths." (Prov. 3:5)

The vow of Obedience, when lived properly, fills the heart with peace, because religious know that, by acting according to obedience, they cannot go astray for they are doing the Will of God.

And what do religious do?

What they **DO** is not as important as what they **ARE**. And that is true of everyone. We should all be concerned with whether we have charity in our heart, are chaste; with whether we are growing in faith, hope, and love; with whether we are becoming more patient, more obedient, more courageous and truthful, more humble and gentle—in short, with whether we are becoming more and more pleasing to God. Then, if we **ARE** the way God has intended us to be, we will **DO** the right thing, which will be good for us, good for others, and give glory to God. We should all be striving to become **SAINTS**. "Be perfect as your heavenly Father is perfect," said Our Lord (Mt 5:48).

Religious spend their day praying and working.

They have a daily schedule that they follow with much care and affection. This schedule—also called "*horarium*" ("ohrareeoom" from the Latin *hora* for "hour")—determines when they are to work, when they are to pray, when they are to study and read, and when they are to relax and talk. By following this schedule each day, religious lead an ordered life that produces much peace and tranquility.

So, according to their schedule, religious stop what they are doing several times a day to go to the chapel to pray where Jesus is in the Blessed Sacrament. Together in the chapel they chant the psalms, read from Holy Scripture and from the writings of the saints, and sing hymns to the glory of God. These periods of prayer observed several times a day make up together what is called "the Divine Office."

And each prayer period has a name, according to when it falls during the day. The three longest and most important of these are Matins, said at night (for some, right at midnight) or at dawn; Lauds, said in the very early morning; and Vespers, said in the early evening.

When the religious are not in the chapel, they are going about their daily chores. But they do not stop praying. In the chapel they pray together in an audible voice. When they leave the chapel, they continue praying in the silence of their hearts, always keeping God in their minds and hearts while they scrub, build, or plough, or cook, or study, or teach, or care for the poor and needy. They are following what St. Paul said: "Pray perseveringly, be attentive to prayer, and pray in a spirit of thanksgiving." (Col. 4:2) We should all do the same thing.

As far as what they **DO**, there are two types of religious. There are "contemplative" religious and there are "active" religious.

Contemplative religious concentrate on prayer. For this they need a life of silence, away from the hustle and bustle of the world. So, all the chores they do take place inside their monastery walls.

Active religious also center their lives in prayer, but they do work with people outside their community, such as teaching children, taking care of the poor, nursing the sick in hospitals, caring for the lonely elderly, and other things that are constructive. Many go out to distant lands, to teach the Gospel to people who have never heard of Jesus Christ, Our Lord, and these are called "missionaries."

But whether they are contemplative or active, all religious imitate the Blessed Virgin Mary and St. Joseph, doing simple things very well for the love of Jesus, with prayer and thanksgiving always humming in their hearts and minds.

And what happens with all this praying and working?

Religious offer all their prayers and all their works, and all their sufferings and all their joys to God the Father, in union with Our Lord Jesus Christ, in order to attain to their own salvation and to obtain grace and salvation for souls, especially the souls of people who do not know or love God. And because of their vows and special promises to God, because of their faithfulness and obedience, through the grace of God they make earth a little closer to Heaven for us all.

THE PRIESTHOOD

Though many men who are religious are also priests, not all priests are religious.

A priest can belong to a religious order, following the horarium and the rules of the religious community, being obedient to the superior of the community. In this case he is a "religious priest." The religious priest wears the habit of the religious order to which he belongs, and he lives in community, inside a monastery or a friary.

Or, a priest can be under the orders of the bishop of a diocese and live in a rectory, or a home attached to a parish church, taking care of the parishioners. In this case he is a "secular priest" or a "diocesan priest." The diocesan priest does not follow an horarium and the rules of a community, since he is not part of a religious community. Instead, he follows the schedule determined by the needs of the parishioners he serves. The diocesan priest wears distinctive clothing, usually black, which shows to people that he is a priest. It is beautiful when the priest wears a "cassock," a long outfit that reaches to the floor, because it reminds us that priests are to be more like angels than like men.

The priesthood is a very special state of being. Through the Sacrament of Ordination, God transforms a man into a priest by giving him the power to do certain things for the salvation of souls as if he were Jesus Christ Himself. He does these things in the person of Christ, and because of this he is, as it were, "another Christ"—an *alter Christus*, as it is said in Latin.

These "certain things" are the sacraments, of which there are seven.* And of these, there are two, besides Baptism, that are most important for our salvation: the Eucharist and Confession. Only a priest can perform the sacraments of the Eucharist and Confession.

Only a priest can do that awesome thing which is to change a little wafer of wheat and some wine in a chalice into the Body and Blood of Christ. He does so at Holy Mass. There, the priest represents Our Lord Jesus Christ in the Last Supper and in His Sacrifice when He died upon the Cross for our sins. When the priest says: "Take this all of you and eat it, for This is My Body" and "Take this all of you and drink of it, for This is My Blood," he says these words in the person of Jesus Christ. *And because of the special powers a priest receives at Ordination*, through him God *transforms* those substances of bread and wine into the Holy Eucharist, which is the Body, Blood, Soul, and Divinity of Christ. This is a very great mystery, to be adored in awe and gratitude. For the Lord said: "He who eats my flesh and drinks my blood has life everlasting, and I will raise him up on the last day. For my flesh is meat indeed and my blood is drink indeed. He that eats my flesh, and drinks my blood abides in me, and I in him." (Jn 6: 55-57)

Through the Holy Spirit a priest also has the power to forgive sins in the person of Christ at the Sacrament of Confession. Jesus Christ conferred this power upon priests when he said: "As the Father has sent me, so I send you. . . . Receive the Holy Spirit! If you forgive men's sins, they are forgiven them; if you hold them bound, they are held bound." (Jn 20: 21-23)

*Baptism, Confirmation, Holy Eucharist, Confession, Matrimony, Holy Orders (or Ordination), Extreme Unction (or Anointing of the Sick).

So you can see that the priesthood is very important, and that is why we should pray for priests every day. The priesthood is a very great gift of God, without which a Christian —religious or lay—cannot attain to *everything* that the Good Lord desires for us. He wishes us to have peace and joy here on earth (despite all our problems), and to be as happy as we can possibly be with Him forever in Heaven (where there are no problems). For this, we must strive to do what He asked of us: to "love God above all things, with all our hearts, and all our souls, and all our minds" and to love our neighbors as ourselves, and to "be perfect as our Father in Heaven is perfect." (Mt. 5: 48) That is, we should strive to become **SAINTS**. And we cannot become saints without continuously uprooting the little (and sometimes big) sins that crop up in our souls, and without feeding ourselves with the heavenly nourishment that is the Body and Blood of Christ, so lovingly given to us at Holy Mass by Christ Himself through his *alter Christus*, the priest.

Let us give thanks and praise to God, Who is so good to us!

29

The religious orders (or families) that we speak of here below are only those that for some reason or another appear in this book. There are many, many other religious orders, such as the Cistercians, the Premonstratensians, the Mercy Fathers, the Visitation nuns, the Brigittine nuns, and so on and so forth. Some religious orders have only men, others have only women, and yet others have both communities of men and communities of women. All have their unique beginnings and history, their own saints, their own customs and way of life (spelled out in a "rule") and their own habit.

BENEDICTINES

St. Benedict (about 480–547) was a wealthy young student in ancient Rome who one day decided to pursue a life of prayer, hidden away in a cave. Before leaving the city for the cave, he made sure his sister, St. Scholastica, was well taken care of. The rest of his possessions he gave away to the poor. What he did in that cave was pray, sing the psalms, read the Scriptures, and dedicate all his labors—whatever they were—to the glory of God. He was very holy and did a lot of good—even from the cave; his fame for holiness soon spread. Others who heard of him came, wanting to join him in the same life of prayer, study, and work—away from the bustle of the world. So St. Benedict left his cave and established a monastery where these men could lead the same kind of life. They prayed and thought of the beauties of God and His creation as they labored the land or did whatever work there was to be done, and studied and read. They got together in their church seven times a day and once in the wee hours of the night to raise their voices in song and prayer. And that is how the Benedictine Order began. These men were called monks.

St. Benedict later wrote down a "rule"—that is, he put down in writing how the monks were to conduct themselves, how they were to pray and live in harmony and holiness. More and more Benedictine monasteries were established and they spread throughout Europe (and later throughout the world) in cities, but mostly out in the country. As the monks started new monasteries, they would bring books with them, and farm tools, and other things that helped build a healthy civilization, while their prayers and sacrifices spread the reign of Our Lord Jesus Christ in souls.

His sister, St. Scholastica, who loved her brother very much, also decided early on to lead the same kind of life with his help. With time, other ladies also followed this way, forming monasteries of Benedictine nuns, spiritual daughters of St. Scholastica.

Though Benedictines may live apart from the world, they pray for the world, and all their prayer and work benefit the world because of their holy way of life. There are Benedictine monks and nuns who also teach and run schools. Benedictines wear a black habit (if it's very hot in the summer, they wear white because that keeps some of the heat away), with a belt around the waist. Over their shoulders, front and back and down beyond their knees, they wear a "scapular" (from the Latin *scapula*, shoulder), which is something like an apron. Many other orders also have the scapular as part of their habit. The men's scapular has a hood. Benedictine nuns wear a veil over their heads, as nuns normally do.

CARMELITES (Order of Our Lady of Mount Carmel)

The Carmelites trace their history way, way back to the time of the prophet Elijah! He lived in a cave on Mount Carmel in the Holy Land, and other men seeking holiness joined him and lived in caves around him as hermits. They used to pray for the coming of the Messiah, and when Jesus Christ, the Messiah, finally came, hermits continued to live on Mount Carmel praying for the spread of His Kingdom. Centuries later, the bishop of Jerusalem, St. Albert (1149–1214), gave them a rule to live by. From there, the Carmelite order spread to Europe and beyond. Because their roots are in the Holy Land, the Carmelites have things related to the Holy Land close to their minds and hearts. They like to think about the Holy Family: the Child Jesus, his mother the Blessed Virgin Mary, and St. Joseph, and how they lived and what they did, including visiting St. Anne, Jesus' grandmother. And then, the hidden life of Jesus growing up, and helping St. Joseph with his carpentry as a young man. And so, they read and meditate (think about) a lot on Scripture passages. The Carmelite order is dedicated to Our Lady of Mount Carmel.

As can happen in life if we are not careful and alert, after a few centuries the Carmelites became a little slack and forgot how to live out their rule. They no longer wore their proper habit and—most seriously—they no longer were attentive to prayer and recollection and a life of simplicity, trusting in God. So in came St. Teresa of Avila (1515–1582), born in Spain, who became a Carmelite nun at the age of 21. She wanted to live a life of greater perfection of soul, very close to Our Lord, and for this she wanted to follow the Carmelite Order's rule just the way it had been written by St. Albert. She started another monastery in order to do that, named after St. Joseph, and other nuns joined her. Soon, some Carmelite friars also went back to living according to the original rule, with St. Teresa's help—the first of whom was St. John of the Cross. Those Carmelites who followed this reformed way of life were called Discalced (without shoes) Carmelites. The nuns are dedicated to a contemplative way of life, strictly dedicated to prayer, and they are "cloistered," meaning they always stay inside the monastery, coming out only to go to doctors and dentists. They pray for everyone, but especially for the Church and for priests.

Carmelites wear a brown habit with a scapular of the same color. At Holy Mass they also wear a white mantle around their shoulders, as well as at the Divine Office on Sundays and solemn days (such as Christmas, Easter, the Annunciation, the Assumption).

CARTHUSIANS

Since time immemorial, there have been souls called to live a life apart, alone, concentrating on being always in conversation with God, curbing the bad tendencies in their souls, and basically fighting against the devil (sometimes even physically!) and putting demons to flight. These are called hermits, and they usually live in isolated places, like deserts or forests, or high up in the mountains. (St. Benedict was a hermit at first, before founding a monastery of monks.)

There was a holy man named Bruno (1030–1101). He was born in Germany and became professor at the School of the Cathedral of Rheims, France. He was very famous and popular, but felt God calling him to leave all that and become a hermit. Bruno also had some friends who had the same inspiration. So, he left his teaching role at Rheims and went with his companions to Grenoble in the Alpine mountains of France, to seek the counsel, or opinion, of the bishop St. Hugh. This holy bishop very much approved of their plan and gave them land in a very isolated mountain, the Chartreuse, from where comes the word "Carthusians" (the "h" got moved somehow).

In the forest on that mountain they built huts for themselves, and would only get together to say the night prayers, being alone with God the rest of the time—praying, studying, doing manual work, growing their own vegetables and the like. And Carthusians still do that, only leaving their little hut (which they also call a cell) for Mass and the evening and night prayers with the community in their monastery church. They wear a white habit with a belt around the waist, and a scapular with a hood. The scapular has a strip of cloth on both sides (called "bands") tied to the front and back. These strips sometimes look like large pockets hanging outside the habit. They symbolize the perpetual bond of the Carthusian monk with God.

CONCEPTIONISTS

The order of Conceptionists is very special because it was established by command of the Blessed Virgin Mary herself to honor her Immaculate Conception! Immaculate Conception means that she was made in her mother's womb without original sin because some day she would give birth to Jesus Christ, Our Lord, whose body can have nothing to do with sin because he is God. Our Lady chose St. Beatriz da Silva (1424–1492), a Portuguese noble-lady, to start the Order of Conceptionists. St. Beatriz was a lady-in-waiting to the Queen of Spain. The queen was jealous of her beauty, gentleness, and wisdom, and one day ordered her to be locked up in a chest hidden in a dungeon. While imprisoned there, St. Beatriz saw Our Lady appear to her, telling her that she would not only survive this ordeal, but would establish a religious order to honor her Immaculate Conception. Our Lady even showed St. Beatriz what type of habit her nuns would use: white, with a white scapular and a blue mantle, and also a medal with an image of Our Lady holding the Baby Jesus.

St. Beatriz waited for the moment when Our Lady would tell her that the time was right. That time came many years afterwards, when there was a new Queen of Spain: Isabel, the Catholic, who helped Columbus discover the Americas. Queen Isabel was a younger cousin of St. Beatriz, and gave her the buildings needed to start the order of Conceptionists. This was in the city of Toledo. Then, some years later, in 1530 when St. Beatriz was already in Heaven, the bishop of Mexico, Bishop Zumarraga, asked Conceptionist nuns to come to that new land in the Americas. He needed nuns to support, by their prayers, the missionary work of the Franciscan friars among the native peoples of Mexico. You may know that it was to this same Bishop Zumarraga that Our Lady of Guadalupe sent roses from Tepeyac hill, which she neatly arranged with her own hands in the "tilma" (mantle) of St. Juan Diego. Our Lady of Guadalupe told St. Juan Diego's uncle (when she came to heal him) that she was the woman "who crushes the serpent's head." Very interesting! That is also how we think of Our Lady under the title (or name) of Immaculate Conception: she crushes the serpent's head—that is, the devil. (Can you find an image of Our Lady of Guadalupe in this book?)

Thus, the Conceptionists were the first religious women to come to the Americas. Among them, the saintly Mother Mariana de Jesús Torres, to whom Our Lady appeared in the early 1600s in Ecuador, making some important revelations about our times. Over the years, the Conceptionists spread throughout Latin America, dedicating their prayers and sacrifices to rescue the people from the wiles of the "serpent"—such as human sacrifice— and bring them to the light and peace of Jesus Christ, Our Lord.

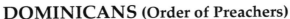

DOMINICANS (Order of Preachers)

As we read in the Bible, from the very beginning of the Church there were misguided people teaching things that were not like what Jesus Christ had taught and His apostles had preached. In the Middle Ages, there was one particularly evil teaching that was spreading quickly, taking people away from the path that leads to peace and joy in God. These people, the Manicheans or Albigensians, taught that "matter"—that is, whatever was physical—was bad and evil, and only the spiritual was good. This is a bit crazy (no?), because God created matter: the seas, the stars, the animals, the trees, fields and flowers, and our own bodies with eyes to see, and nose to smell, and ears to hear. Some Albigensians went so far as to even say that it was best to kill the body so that the spirit could be free to fly away. Crazy. But many people were falling for this and being led to confusion, rebellion, and darkness. So God sent St. Dominic to go about the streets preaching the Truth and Light of the Gospel.

St. Dominic de Guzmán was a Spaniard (1170–1221), but most of his preaching was done in southern France, where the Albigensians were strong. He was extremely bright and used very good reasoning. But he was also very holy. He prayed, read, and meditated on the Bible, and offered penances and deprivations to God (like fasting). And through all this, people started coming back to the true Faith.

There was a group of young and older women who had actually been following the wrong way of the Albigensians and were converted to the true Faith by St. Dominic. They told him that they wanted to become nuns and be totally dedicated to God in the True Faith, and pray for those who were still living in darkness and error. St. Dominic helped them with that, "founding" (starting) a community of Dominican nuns. Like St. Dominic, they prayed and fasted for the conversion of Albigensians. No wonder they brought so many people back to the Catholic Faith! With time, other men joined St. Dominic in his work of preaching—priests and brothers—and that is how the Dominican Order, also known as the Order of Preachers, came about.

Dominicans are very good teachers. They are especially dedicated to the Rosary, since St. Dominic prayed it daily and preached its use as a weapon against the devil. They wear a white habit with white scapular, a black cope around the shoulders, and a belt with a rosary that hangs on the left side where, in the Middle Ages, soldiers used to carry their swords.

FRANCISCANS

St. Francis of Assisi (about 1181–1226) was the son of a wealthy Italian merchant. He had great ambitions of becoming rich and famous, and would go to battle and participate in jousts in order to conquer fame. But one day God touched his heart when he ran into a leper. Behind the unsightly deformed features of the man who stood begging in front of him was a soul that Our Lord had redeemed and loved very much, a soul needy not only of food, but of love. This made St. Francis reflect about life; and he changed. He turned his attention to God and to singing His praises, instead of seeking to be praised himself. And he abandoned all his cares to God. He didn't want to have anything of his own, but rather to be free as the birds in the air and the lilies of the field, depending entirely on God the Father's providence. He renounced his rights to his merchant father's riches, even the clothes he had on, and retired to an old abandoned church to live for God and trust in Him. And he started rebuilding the church. He had nothing of his own, and depended on the charity and help of others. Then more and more men joined him, and this is how the Franciscan Order began.

Many in the Church at that time had forgotten the ways of the Gospel: being God's friend, doing what He tells us, and trusting in His providence. Through his preaching—but especially through his example—St. Francis called people back to the Christian way of life.

Besides Franciscan friars, there are also Franciscan sisters. They may teach, or work at hospitals, or do many other different things for the good of others. The habit of the Franciscans is typically brown, but there are some branches of the Franciscan family that use grey, and others use black. Regardless of whatever color they use, they always have a white cord around the waist and a rosary tied to it. They do not wear scapulars. (Notice the cord has three knots, representing the three vows of chastity, poverty, and obedience.) Franciscan men are called friars, and their habit always has a hood.

POOR CLARES

The Poor Clares are actually part of the Franciscan Order and were founded by St. Francis and St. Clare of Assisi (1194–1253). St. Clare was very beautiful and gracious, and there were many young men seeking her hand in marriage. However, one day she heard St. Francis preaching in the cathedral of Assisi in very simple words, talking about God and what joy and freedom there is in being detached from the things of this world, both inwardly and outwardly. She put aside her rich clothes and sparkling jewels, and left her family's palace to live in poverty in a convent, trusting in God alone, praying for others and for the Church even as she went about her daily chores. Soon other young ladies joined her—even her own sister, Agnes. And after St. Clare's father passed away, her mother, Ortolana, also joined. And that is how the Poor Clares began.

Poor Clare nuns are dedicated to contemplative prayer and are cloistered, like Carmelite nuns. They wear a habit similar to the Franciscan friars': brown, with the white cord and rosary. And because they are women, they add the veil, with the wimple (a cloth covering the neck and head). The Poor Clares go about barefooted.

MISSIONARIES OF CHARITY

The Missionaries of Charity were founded in 1950 by Saint Teresa of Calcutta (1910–1997), better known as Mother Teresa of Calcutta. Mother Teresa felt the call to religious life when she was still young. She joined an order of teaching sisters—the Loreto Sisters—and was sent to India to teach children there. One day, in 1946, while on a train ride to her annual retreat, she felt a very strong call to bring souls to Jesus by serving the poorest of the poor: the many people who had nothing to eat, nowhere to call their home, and nowhere even to die in peace. As always happens in a work of God, others felt called to the same mission and joined Mother Teresa. In 1950, Pope Pius XII gave her permission to establish a religious order—the Missionaries of Charity—which has now spread all throughout the world. The habit of the sisters is a white sari (the typical dress of a lady in India) with three blue stripes at the edge in honor of Our Lady, and a cross at the left shoulder.

REDEMPTORISTS
(Congregation of the Holy Redeemer)

Jesus told his apostles and disciples to take the Gospel to the far ends of the world, and that is what they—and those who followed them—did. They would go to different cities and preach in public places and in homes, and from those cities the Faith spread. But sometimes, people living out in the countryside, faraway from churches and priests, didn't learn the Faith or they became forgetful of it. St. Alphonsus Liguori (1696–1787) had these people in mind when he founded the Redemptorists, or the Congregation of the Holy Redeemer, in his native southern Italy. The main mission of Redemptorist priests was to go to a place (usually a far away village), stay there for some days or a week or more, and preach to the people in that area in order to bring them back to the practice of their Faith—help them discover the glories and the love of God, repent of their sins that sadden Him, and find grace and strength in the sacraments, especially Confession and the Holy Eucharist. Like other important religious orders, they grew and grew, and Redemptorist priests still preach missions throughout the world. The habit of the Redemptorist is an ancient form of the cassock (the long black tunic worn by some priests) with a white collar visible all around the neck with an opening in front. They have a cincture (a wide belt) around the waist, and a full rosary wound around the cincture. They also wear a crucifix inside their habit and a larger one tucked into the cincture when on mission.

LITTLE SISTERS OF THE POOR

One day, St. Jeanne Jugan (1792–1879) was walking down the streets of Saint-Servan (a small town in northwestern France) and saw a very elderly, blind lady just lying there with no one to care for her. She picked her up in her own arms and took her into her little apartment, laying the elderly lady on her own bed. Soon she brought another elderly lady in, and another, and her roommates and friends joined in to help. St. Jeanne already lived a quiet life of prayer while working to make a living and helping needy people. Now, with her friends, she organized the little group into a religious order, writing a "rule of life" for them, approved by the Church. And that is how the Little Sisters of the Poor began. Today the sisters continue taking care of the elderly, running homes where they can live well, always with a chapel down the hall. Most importantly, the sisters help them prepare for that great day when they will pass away into Eternity and meet their Lord and God.

JESUITS (Society of Jesus)

St. Ignatius of Loyola (1491–1556) was a soldier in northern Spain, full of worldly ambitions of glory, until a cannonball hit his legs in a battle doing great damage to one of them. That leg never quite healed very well, but his soul was transformed by the healing graces of the mercy of God. While he was recovering at a castle, all he could do was lie in bed and read the only two books to be found there: a book of the lives of the saints, and a book entitled *Life of Jesus Christ.* Through these readings— and aware of his helpless condition—he discovered that it is much more glorious and honorable to serve the King of Kings, God Almighty, than an earthly king. So that is what he set out to do once he had recovered. He went to the University of Paris (France) to learn more about the Faith, and then, with a few companions, went to Rome, where he started the Society of Jesus, also called the Jesuit Order. The core mission of the Jesuits has always been to teach, and especially to teach the Catholic faith, particularly to those who are confused about it or have never heard of it. That is why the Jesuit Order sent missionaries to the farthest lands, such as St. Francis Xavier (1506–1552) to India and Japan, and St. Jean de Brébeuf (1593–1649) and St. Isaac Jogues (1607–1646) to the Hurons and other native nations in the US and Canada. Jesuits also have schools.

Here follows an explanation of the people you see in the pages about the Religious Vows.

VOW OF POVERTY

St. Francis of Assisi had nothing of his own, and depended on the charity and help of others. He was just as happy eating stale bread as he was eating a good meal, accepting both as coming from the hands of God. He became known as the "Poverello," the "little poor man" in Italian. (See the story of the Franciscan Order above.) In the picture, you can see the five "stigmata." In a mysterious way, Our Lord Jesus Christ imprinted His own wounds in St. Francis's hands, feet, and side (as happened with St Padre Pio in 1918). This was a sign of the great union that St. Francis had with Jesus, to the point of sharing in His sufferings.

St. Clare of Assisi, following St. Francis' example, put aside her beautiful dresses to wear a rough habit and live in very simple surroundings. She and her sisters in religion (that is, the other nuns who lived in the same monastery with her) would wash and scrub and keep everything very clean, and mend their habits so they would last as long as possible. She was very happy for not being attached to things. (See the story of the Poor Clares above.)

Pope Benedict XVI said about St. Francis and St. Clare: ". . . those who do the Lord's will and trust in him alone lose nothing; on the contrary, they find the true treasure that can give meaning to all things." [Letter on the Eighth Centenary of the foundation of the Poor Clares, April 1, 2012]

VOW OF CHASTITY

St. Aloysius Gonzaga (1568–1591) was of a noble family of northern Italy. His father was an important military commander who wanted his son to be a soldier too. When he was only four (!), his father took St. Aloysius to stay with him where a battalion was preparing for war so that the young boy could start learning. He liked it very much, and was becoming a little soldier. But along with that he picked up some not-so-good language and manners. This started changing when he became ill, at eight years of age. He then turned to reading biographies of saints and to prayer, and so started regretting the bad words and his rough manners. With the encouragement of the castle's chaplain and his own mother, he changed his ways. More and more, he wanted to be alone to talk with God and read Holy Scripture, and think in his heart about all the beautiful things God created. Even though he played with princes, and lived in courts, and accompanied his parents when they visited kings and queens, he was never lured by the fancy things of this world. He wanted to be away from distractions, with his mind always on heavenly things, and kept his eyes low so as not to see ugly behavior that could disturb his peace. As he grew older, he realized God was indeed calling him to be a soldier, but a soldier for Christ. He became a Jesuit in the Society of Jesus. (See the story of the Jesuits above.)

St. Thérèse of the Child Jesus (1873–1897) was born in France. Her parents were very devout (Saints Louis and Zélie Martin) and as a consequence, she and her four sisters grew up very focused on Our Lord and Our Lady, and the things of God. Though she was a bit stubborn and whining as a little girl, she learned to conquer these traits with the help of her family, but most especially through prayer and reflection, and the grace of God. Very early she wanted to give herself entirely to living for God alone, and entered the Carmelite Order when she was only 15! She loved our Lord Jesus with such a great love, and everything she did—the tiniest thing—she did with great care to make Him happy.

VOW OF OBEDIENCE

In the early days of the Benedictine Order, there were young boys and teenagers who were little monks. St. Benedict watched over and cared for them as a father. One day little St. Placid went down to the lake to fetch some water with a bucket. He ended up being swept into the lake by the water current and was very close to drowning. St. Benedict, inside the monastery, knew in his heart that this was happening. He ordered the young monk St. Maurus to run to the lake and pull St. Placid out of the water. After asking for a blessing and receiving it, St. Maurus dashed off with all his might. He was so intent on his mission that he didn't even notice, when he got to the lake, that he was running on water! He reached St. Placid, pulled him out, and ran back to the margins of the lake carrying him. Only when they were all safe and sound, standing on firm ground, did St. Maurus realize he had walked on water, just like St. Peter had done centuries before. It was his obedience to his spiritual father and religious superior St. Benedict that brought about this miracle and saved little St. Placid's life.

St. Rita of Cascia (1381–1457) was called to be a nun of the Augustinian Order, which follows a rule written by St. Augustine of Hippo (354–430). She entered an Augustinian convent in Cascia, Italy, when she was already an older woman. While St. Rita was a novice, Mother Superior wanted to test her obedience. She ordered St. Rita to plant a dead stick and water it every day. To us this would seem a great waste of time and water, and a rather silly thing to do. But St. Rita did exactly what her mother superior told her to do, with much sweetness and love because she was doing it for Jesus. Well, lo and behold: after a while, the dead stick began showing signs of life! It put out a little green shoot here, and another there, and then little leaves started coming out, and with time, the dead stick became a beautiful rose bush, which still blooms to this very day.

PRAYER FOR PRIESTS*

O Jesus, Eternal Priest, keep Your priests within the shelter of Your Sacred Heart, where none may touch them. Keep unstained their anointed hands which daily touch Your Sacred Body. Keep unsullied their lips, daily purpled with Your Precious Blood. Keep pure and unworldly their hearts, sealed with the sublime mark of Your Priesthood. Let Your holy love surround them from the world's contagion. Bless their labors with abundant fruit. May the souls to whom they minister be their joy and consolation here, and their everlasting crown hereafter. Amen.

*Prayer said every day by St. Thérèse of Lisieux from her childhood on.

GLOSSARY

Monk: Monks are men of those religious orders that were originally founded as contemplative communities to live apart from the world, concentrating on prayer, study, and manual labor—that is, "monastic orders": Benedictines (and all other orders that came from the Benedictine Order, such as the Cistercians, Trappists, Calmadolese, etc.), Carthusians, etc.

Friar: Generally speaking, friars are men of religious orders that were founded in the High Middle Ages with some specific active purpose in society or a particular charism, usually called "mendicant" orders because its members used to beg for their food: Carmelites, Dominicans, Franciscans, Mercedarians (founded in 1218 to redeem Christian captives enslaved by Muslims), and Servites (founded in 1233 to propagate devotion to the Blessed Virgin Mary, Mother of God).

Nun: Nuns are women who belong to religious orders—or branches of these orders—that are contemplative in nature and purpose. Often they are cloistered, such as the Carmelites and Poor Clares.

Sister: Sisters are women who belong to active religious orders, performing charitable functions such as caring for the sick, the poor, and also teaching. Some active orders are the Missionaries of Charity, the Little Sisters of the Poor, the Sisters of Life (in the US).

Brother is the title used to address religious men who are not priests.

Father is the title used to address priests, whether religious or diocesan.

Sister is the title used to address all women religious, whether nuns or active sisters.

Religious Superiors:
"Abbot" (men) or "Abbess" (women) is the title used for religious superiors in monastic orders. Prior is the second-in-command, and Subprior is the third-in-command in a monastic community.

The title "Prior" or "Prioress" is used in "mendicant" orders (see above) for their religious superiors. The second-in-command is a Subprior or Subprioress. Franciscan friars, however, call their religious superiors "Father Guardian," and Poor Clares use the term "Abbess" for their superiors.

Religious superiors in orders founded after the Middle Ages are usually called "Father Superior" or "Mother Superior."

U I O G D

Ut in omnia glorificetur Deus.

That in all things God may be glorified.

Printed in the USA
CPSIA information can be obtained
at www.ICGtesting.com
LVHW071526270823
756425LV00019B/776